AF270679

Sloth

by Grace Hansen

Abdo Kids Jumbo is an Imprint of Abdo Kids
abdobooks.com

abdobooks.com

Published by Abdo Kids, a division of ABDO, P.O. Box 398166, Minneapolis, Minnesota 55439.
Copyright © 2023 by Abdo Consulting Group, Inc. International copyrights reserved in all countries.
No part of this book may be reproduced in any form without written permission from the publisher.
Abdo Kids Jumbo™ is a trademark and logo of Abdo Kids.

Printed in the United States of America, North Mankato, Minnesota.

052022

092022

THIS BOOK CONTAINS
RECYCLED MATERIALS

Photo Credits: Alamy, Getty Images, Minden Pictures, Shutterstock

Production Contributors: Teddy Borth, Jennie Forsberg, Grace Hansen
Design Contributors: Candice Keimig, Victoria Bates

Library of Congress Control Number: 2021950568
Publisher's Cataloging-in-Publication Data

Names: Hansen, Grace, author.

Title: Sloth / by Grace Hansen.

Description: Minneapolis, Minnesota : Abdo Kids, 2023 | Series: South American animals | Includes online
     resources and index.

Identifiers: ISBN 9781098261856 (lib. bdg.) | ISBN 9781098262693 (ebook) | ISBN 9781098263119
     (Read-to-Me ebook)

Subjects: LCSH: Sloths--Juvenile literature. | Mammals--Behavior--Juvenile literature. | South America
     Juvenile literature. | Rain forest animals--Juvenile literature. | Zoology--Juvenile literature.

Classification: DDC 599.313--dc23

Table of Contents

South America

South America is filled with lovely landscapes, from rain forests to mountain ranges. Because of these special places, a **diverse** group of animals live on the **continent**. Sloths are just some of these animals.

5

Sloths

Sloths live throughout Central and South America. There are six different **species** of sloth. They are split into two groups. There are two-toed and three-toed sloths.

Three-toed sloth
Two-toed sloth
7

Other than their toes, sloths look very much the same. They have long legs. Their heads are round. They have tiny ears.

Brown-throated
three-toed sloth

A sloth's fur can be gray, black, or brown depending on its **species**. Three-toed sloths have special coloring on their face. It makes it look like they are smiling.

Sloths move very slowly. Some hang upside down for most of the day. Others tuck themselves into forks in trees.

Linnaeus's
two-toed sloth

Because sloths don't move much, **algae** grow on their fur. This makes sloths look green in color. It helps them blend in with the trees.

Food

Sloths like to eat anything they can find up in trees. They eat fruits and other parts of plants. Sometimes they will eat insect **larvae** and bird eggs.

Baby Sloths

Sloths are **solitary** animals. They only come together to have young. A female gives birth to one baby.

19

A baby holds onto its mother anywhere from 5 weeks to 6 months. Then it is ready to be on its own. The baby will remain near its mother for up to four years.

More Facts

- Sloths sleep for up to 20 hours a day. When they are awake, they don't move much.

- Sloths are surprisingly very good swimmers!

- Sloths come down to the ground once every 6 or 7 days. This is so they can go to the bathroom. They move along the forest floor by pulling themselves with their front claws.

Glossary

algae – organisms that live mainly in the water and make their food through photosynthesis. Algae are different from other plants in that they have no true leaves, roots, or stems.

continent – one of the earth's seven major areas of land. The continents are Africa, Antarctica, Asia, Australia, Europe, North America, and South America.

diverse – of different kinds or sorts.

larva – an insect after it hatches from an egg and before it changes into its adult form.

solitary – living without others.

species – a group of living things that look alike and can have young together.

Index

Abdo Kids
ONLINE
FREE! ONLINE MULTIMEDIA RESOURCES

Visit **abdokids.com** to access crafts, games, videos, and more!

Use Abdo Kids code
SSK1856
or scan this QR code!